Convertible Night, Flurry of Stones

Books by Dzvinia Orlowsky

Convertible Night, Flurry of Stones

poems by Dzvinia Orlowsky

Carnegie Mellon University Press
Pittsburgh 2008

Acknowledgments

These poems have appeared, sometimes in different versions, in the following publications:

American Poetry Review: "Cheap"
Field: "Ballet on Chemo"
Shade: "Owl, Cyva," "Who Forgives Whom"
Pebble Lake Review: "Nude Descending," "The Way Water Falls," "Losing My Hair"
Salamander: "Night Shift," "Convertible Night"
AGNI: "Infusion," "*Carpe Diem*"
PoetryRepairShop: "The Radiologist," "Kabalevsky's Concerto," "White Orchard," "Lava Lamp," "Octave"
The Drunken Boat: "Good Cells," "The Cop," "Another Waiting Room," "December," "Wolves," "Yes, Back," "*All Gone*"
The Wild River Review: "Sea Gull," "The Fitting," "Tulips," "Listening to Schumann's Piano Concerto"
Ward 6 Review: "Arc," "Watching," "Paper Cut," "First Rain"

"Nude Descending" appeared in *Pushcart Prize XXXI*

"Losing My Hair" appeared in *Never Before: Poems about First Experiences*, edited by Laure-Anne Bosselaar (Four Way Books, 2006).

"Who Forgives Whom" also appeared in the Cervena Barva Press Postcard Series (2005).

With all my love to Jay, Max, and Raisa, my bright daylight. With much appreciation to my healers; there were many of you; to Lee Hope and our writers' community for their generous caring and support; to Gary Duehr and Nancy Mitchell for their invaluable comments; to Nancy, in particular, for her friendship and encouragement from the first moment of diagnosis to and beyond the first words of this book. And last but not least, my gratitude to Jerry Costanzo, Cynthia Lamb, and the Carnegie Mellon staff for their support throughout the years.

Book design: Michael Szczerban
Author photo: Jay Hoffman
Publication of this book is supported by a grant from the Pennsylvania Council on the Arts.

Library of Congress Control Number: 2007931372
ISBN-13: 978-0-88748-482-7 Pbk.

10 9 8 7 6 5 4 3 2 1

PENNSYLVANIA
COUNCIL
ON THE
ARTS

Contents

For my sister, Maria,
my positive half

Prologue

Pink,

my arm held
under hot running water,

blue vein bulge, trumpet sound—

Carnival flower, five fingers ready to dance.
Release the elastic!

They want to start a life of their own:

thumb, orphaned
nail, bleached hillside.

Blood disposed down a drain—
my name, street, best time to be reached.

Good Will

A neighbor weaves a pink ribbon
through our white picket fence,

embellishes a bleak spot of lawn
with a sad girl copper statuette

holding a potted pink geranium.
Now everyone knows.

I

*But the very hairs of your head
are all numbered.*

—Matthew 10:30

Listening to Schumann's Piano Concerto

That we don't all die in childhood
is the greater miracle,

God lifting His light hand
to bring out a phrase, clearing the pedal.

We wear our jewels for the afternoon,
startle birds with the immensity

of our human shadows.
We've made it to hard chairs.

Restlessly our hands roll program notes
into telescopes; we intercept genius

with our signature cough.
But what is to be known of great music

other than it requires black polished shoes
and silence,

the incontestable desire to sleep?
See how our mouths relax into soft wax,

our faces drip down our throats.
This is what it must feel like to be lovingly held.

Hear how beauty begs forgiveness
for not including us.

Ultrasound

1.

Months ago, my hand lifted blindly
toward my body,
as if to say Grace
at the notch of its granite wall.

Lightly my fingers circled,
oblivious to the flash thunder
and lightning of the muted TV.

Outside, summer's
last blossoming rise,
black pinholes
pierced through its pink petals.
Some thing had failed
at fully tasting it.

How readily the body's cells
insist upon their Braille,
a single, tiny doorknob—

2.

All winter, I ate only what had skin,
black-threaded, pocked,
citrus split into glass,
tiny orange flecks.

I saw the pity in the eyes of neighbors.
Lucky not to be me, although they, too, had
had close calls.

Each offered words like food
I couldn't swallow.

3.

Drugged, I sang to it, turning the key
on the small white lace musical pillow
given at birth to my son

by a man now dust.
Its quivering mechanical pitches
played against my bruised skin,

the deepening twilight yellow
from the biopsy needle.

4.

The nurse technician arched the cold mouse
freely over my gelled skin.
Are you warm enough?

Her steady voice
reminded me to lie still
as she wiped my breast clean.

After that she gave me a little extra time
to slide off the table,

a little extra time to get dressed,

a little extra time to place her hand
on my shoulder,

a little extra time for the door to open
a little extra wide.

The Radiologist

after Franz Kafka

He calls again to confirm what's already been confirmed.
You do not have to leave the room.

Still, he's hungry for conversation—as if you'd become his friend
Remain standing in your place and listen.

over the stiff shot of bad news. You have to listen to him
Do not even listen, simply wait.

fearful he'll add centimeters to the tumor, just to be safe.
Do not even wait.

But tonight he wants you to know more: you're practically
Be quiet, still and solitary.

neighbors. And did I know, he continues, that the house
The world will freely offer itself to you

with the 35 acres, just off the town's most desirable street,
To be unmasked.

was his. Isn't it a coincidence that his daughter, too,
It has no choice.

is a writer. Only she's with a bigger, New York City house.
It will roll in ecstasy at your feet.

Maybe I'd like to buy a signed copy of her book someday.
You do not have to leave the room.

Everything's blessed and enlarged in his family's life:
Remain standing in your place and listen.

his daughter's gratitude for wildflowers, the easy country
Do not even listen, simply wait.

she grew up in, his immeasurable love for her.
Do not even wait.

And all I want to ask again is *just how big* and if he's completely certain.
    Be quiet, still and solitary.

But he's through talking and hangs up.
    The world will freely offer itself to you

If it wasn't for my love of God, his mud-soft meadows,
    To be unmasked.

I'd drive my green Ford through the doctor's brambles and dead ends,
    It has no choice.

I'd find his blossoming daughter
    It will roll in ecstasy at your feet.

and take her life.

Night Shift

The doctor presses my fingers
against hard wooden beads
too large to be a rosary.
This, he teaches me,
is what cancer feels like.

On the small TV, Jimi Hendrix
bends the note on his Fender so far it weeps.
If blood could change hands,
I'd join the party gathering
outside my door—
night shift nurses
new as daffodils.

There are no stairs,
only a voice that lifts and carries,
tells me *imagine the future pocket side*,
customized silk, fitted and stitched
the blue of my eyes.

If I Can Feel the World Tonight,

I won't
force myself
to love
myself
but rather the spare stars
above the hospital's parking garage.

I Wasn't Aware

for Maria

of friends
each who took a stone
and threw it out
as far
as was possible

past a collapsed train
of shopping carts,
out of a car window,
passing a freezing pond
into nearby woods,
across a neighbor's circular
driveway, through a stop sign,
toward the ocean, past the sun-bleached,
vacant lifeguard's chair

threw it out
as far
as was possible
from me.

The Way Water Falls

The falling water plays my right
numbed, wooden side,

irreparably separate,
buzzing slack pitches like strings

on a Spanish guitar.
I'll gladly forget how it hammers

my body's newly veneered surface,
the cut, trenched and sealed.

Let it play a chord I've never
heard before, the first passage

of grass at the end of pain.
The warmth invites my scar to bleed.

I rub it gently.
It bleeds more.

A small trail runs down my waist,
along my inner thigh to the drain

where it slowly pools, blooms
like a rose at my feet.

I hold the guitar closer,
allow its implausible terms.

Infusion

Two clowns step off the elevator
with crowded, static-angry

balloons tied to their wrists
just as the hospital cafeteria

shuts down. You redirect them
to the children's floor.

But the children don't want them either.
They have suffered enough good cheer—

as have the well-meaning clowns,
trying for just one laugh

with their large plastic combs
and bungle-stuffed catchall satchels.

After all, *you're* the one with the sad face.
Somehow, despite the cool reception,

they stick around
secretly glad not to be you.

They tell you hair comes back,
pointing to the screaming red

flames just above their ears.
You may as well love a pet rat,

the way it worries in morning light
and in the afternoon,

how it nightly attempts to decode
with practiced hands

a clump of dirt
before taking it into its mouth.

Let it circle your neck,
run its tail across your open mouth.

Laughter, isn't it *the best medicine?*
Yes, keep laughing.

It's dragged its tail
through much worse.

Losing My Hair

It fills my hand
like a small animal,
species unknown.

I could name it,
close my eyes, rub it gently
against my face

tangled in my fingers,
soft as silk from a cornfield.

Look, look—I call to my husband
carrying it down the stairs.

Not that I wasn't warned by doctors
that one day I'd find it
on my pillows,
in the drain,
on my plate,
in my food.

That morning it started to snow,
nothing that'd cover the ground well enough—

black splintered branches,
strewn all over the yard,

neither wind nor trees.

***

I couldn't bear to wrap it in toilet paper,
throw it out.

I carried some strands to the woods,
spread them on the ground

for the birds to lift
into their nests.

I placed some more strands
in an empty hornet's nest,

its gray center welcoming
my hand.

The hornets were gone,
but the birds might come back.

I wrapped the last few strands with some horsehair I'd kept.
A few thick pieces of a black mane

I'd pulled riding once, out of fear.

    ***

Donna, the hairstylist, turns on
the electric clippers,
says *Hon, do me a favor*
and close your eyes.

She's tall, heavy,
and sweet as sugar,
hair a teased peroxide
blond beehive.

Over the phone she'd said
not to worry about anything,

they had wigs—
they would play with me.

    ***

The first wig makes me look
like an airline ticketing agent.

The second one drives a school bus.
The third one, curling around my mouth,

wants sex. That one couldn't be worn
near an open oven door.

The dark one, like my mother's hair,
loves the rain,

travels well in a small box.
Donna says *Try this human hair,*

it fits like a silk glove.
But it's short, thick, Oriental hair,

a gold medallist, figure skater's hair.
Donna says the reason my complexion looks so sallow

is because of all the chemo.
I leave the yellow of her fitting room.

Sweeping the floor
around my chair, Donna says

After the eyelashes and eyebrows go,
your eyes will need more bang.

Another Waiting Room

after Elizabeth Bishop

The breasts here, too, are horrifying,
lit by the same master-plan bulb
that could bleach our teeth, our skulls
long before we're buried.

Some, I imagine, emit an inaudible scream.
Mine, I thought, small enough to be left alone.
The mammogram plate lifts and presses
until I can't breathe,

until the technician's convinced
she's clasped everything on metal.
It's skin that holds us all together,
soft and dreadful.

I turn my face until I can't look any further
to see what it was I was—*a fine black thread
still crimped from the strain and snap.*
I'm back in it.

Outside it's cold, snowing.
The floor rises up in my throat.
My body dissolves into a million grains
to be ciphered by a passing wind.

I don't know what's been written
in the yellow margins
after she's through and I'm returned
like a weeping child to myself.

Nude Descending

Be broken in bright light,
a drain in your back, your body
releasing its deepest red,
a cardinal opening a wing
within. Halved, one side soft,
the other, a scar running
like a railroad track up to your underarm
where your life was spared, that open
field of broken glass and bad boys
who'd slit anyone's skin just for the thrill,
just as the doctor appeared, asked you
to count backwards. Be shattered
walking the hospital corridor, slowly,
as each nurse changes her face, name,
smiles and pretends to know you.
Be just at the top of God knows what list,
turn toward a mirror and see all fire,
know your name spills like coal.
Be broken in your car, watch
the light snowfall gather
on the car's hood, disappear;
dream of eating only air.
Stand at the top of the stairs,
in light falling from the high window.
Be fractured, discharged, come down
lightly as the first snowfall
white points, torches in your hands.

II

Down their carved names the rain-drop ploughs.

—Thomas Hardy,
"During Wind and Rain"

Who Forgives Whom

Who forgives whom in the moment
of slow ascending, lifted from the body

badly bruised for a sigh,
in that moment less than sacred

when there are no bidders
no God disguised in bright kids' clothes,

singing, pushing a stroller down the sidewalk
into a crack.

All morning, the sky lets go
of what it no longer harbors:

long needles of lightning,
the fugitive blue.

Whose eyes enter ours,
each breath a bird leaving our bodies,

never claiming to know holy
or cry out for it?

Octave

1.

What song was it
        that carried me from childhood

to a large silver frame where I took on
        my grandmother's grave face?

I remember her hands,
        a worried knot of prayer

immersed in a washbasin of ice water—-
        Did she believe she held

an arctic ocean there, imperceptible waves
        that would return her missing son,

absolve the orphan
        she insisted I was?

2.

Long afternoons brought the comfort
        of her large breasts

against a summer cotton dress.
        My knees tucked, gathered into her lap,

I watched the rainbow
        glint off the needle, thread

appearing and swirling, her arm in sunlight,
        conducting.

3.

Mother insisted I kiss Grandmother's hands
      placed across the crucifix,

fingers draped like seaweed,
      mute, still.

Mother lifted me into the satin-lined boat,
      although I pushed back,

turned away, the rubber soles of my shoes
      braced hard

against the unforgiving wooden sides.
      I can't remember when I finally gave in,

allowed my lips to touch
      her air-conditioned skin.

4.

Before the radiologist called on our cell phone
      as we drove toward the ocean,

I saw a church sign that read:
      Remember the promise of the rainbow.

The doctor advised to pull off the side of the road,
      Pull my children closer.

one under each arm.
      I remember their crying,

how a single thread
      pierced the blue sky, lifted my face.

5.

Grandmother, your son did survive
    the years in Siberia.

He did come to America.
    to stand at your grave.

The Bolshevik soldiers who lifted
    their guns to fire on him

are now only this cornfield, wind-rustled,
    in blond uniform

in late-summer Ohio. Grandmother,
    my own son has asked me

Can I go with you? I promise you

    I will not take him
    or my daughter
    or my husband.

I wash my face with cold water.
    My hair grows back like black stubble

shadowed in the winter field
    where you and I once walked.

Let it begin, now,
    let it begin to snow.

Kabalevsky's Concerto

for Max

Think of something sad; the music will come,
his piano teacher tells him.
Now he must consider the way
the melody sinks rather than lifts,
nudges a blister through his young skin.
The room's lampshade turns a dirty brown.
A sea gull rises above the piano's black shore.
His horse, weary, refuses to turn back;
so what if his mother is unable to keep up.
That's what beauty requires.
So what if his mother can't ride a horse.
Poor woman, eyes deep and soulful as onions,
slogging through the deepening snow.

Books Randomly Opened

and left for dead.
Their words wait to move

off the watchful white,
breath without melody

outside the body.
Everything wants to be freed

from inherent predisposition,
lives startled, closed, before

they've begun to speak.
I have laid facedown, felt

the dark river of my spine
pass to stone. My blood

flows generously, tapped
near my weakest finger.

Among the black reeds rushing to red,
on the page it might spell *stop*.

First Rain

In the dark basement, someone
elbowed me hard through the cloud

of my cotton candy dress.
The first heavy rain was about to fall.

Plastic swans wouldn't glide on a paper tablecloth,
their backs filled with salty peanuts.

There was cake, candles easily snapped,
flames escaping toward the ceiling.

Why was everyone leaving?
No stopped music yet, no last chairs.

Prayer to My Father

I couldn't bear your pain, so I wished out loud
I could take it away from you.

On the anniversary of your death,
recently diagnosed, maybe God took me

literally and it's just taken this long
for you to open your eyes and see me.

When you drew a deep breath
I believed I was beautiful,

the way you took my hands, thanked me
for taking the long flight home.

I stayed for weeks although
I heard nothing rise above your silence,

fields of wild white daisies.
They did not darken.

Twenty-five years later,
my blood carries everything you refused.

Watching

The last time I held clover to my face
there was only earth,

a clear sky and in the distance
a young goat crying like a child,

its horns stuck in a wire fence,
head like a large hourglass.

These were our family's ten acres
of meadow grass, the sound

of my parents young and beautiful
preparing for a party;

the hush of my mother's
low-cut velvet dress sliding

past her shoulders
as she leaned her hips against

the bar; in my father's hands,
an iced gimlet shaker, maracas.

Later, everyone's joke was funny,
laughter pitched to the ceiling

and out through the window
to where I was always lying

in the grass, watching my parents
glide through the party like paper dolls.

They've become so small
they buzz when I lift them to my face.

Arc

Father, you heaved open the cellar doors
surprised by your weight and strength,
mice scurrying past your feet.

You found a cat's skull,
a canary's beak, a whistle,
a child's metal shovel,

and clothes, dresses—so many,
a doll with a rubber band
tight around its arm.

For years I wondered where
you'd find me, paired
for this life, your spitting image.

Yes, Back

Hastily pre-dye-shampooed in the afternoon queue, some strands
turn deep sapphire blue. She calls it *yes, black.*

Others twirl stray silver tape down her neck, the color of
withered shingles outside of her new room, not the home she

refused to leave, where undesignated envelopes returned, marked:
better address needed. Her dreams answer: *yes, back.*

She points to her calendar, then to the clock. She remembers
clearly which daughter never comes on time and which leaves early.

My sister brings her walking shoes, I bring her my one
month of recovery, my *Joan of Arc Released before the Fire.*

She lifts a paper place mat to show us how carefully she has drawn
a vase of flowers with a thick black crayon like the one she used years ago,

the light gray appearing like endangered dune grass.
The bottle touches its point to her white skin, uneven lines,

attempts to color in the shoreline just above her eyes.
Yes, they pull me in, their *back, black.*

Cheap

There was still enough time
to have turned toward each other,
arms open, before turning away
the way families sometimes do,

each sister suffering more than the other.
None of that crossed our minds,
ever struck *bingo* in the dining hall,
pennies moved slowly and deliberately

like battleships. So we reinvented love,
allowed hate to prickle, bitch blossomed
in a plastic vase. Bad thoughts
swarmed like fat, garbage-fed,

late-August flies. After all,
Mother's fire-proofed banking chest,
never locked, opened freely
to a single dollar bill

lying undisturbed on green felt.
Did you find the money?
she'd ask, chuckling to herself,
her recently dyed hair

combed straight up.
Yes, I answered, *all of it . . . thank you.*
I hated leaving her fragile
hands working the wheelchair,

pushing hard. Coming was easier,
Mother flowing into the morning
current downstream to the door.
Outside, the ocean promised fish,

the summer sun warm as beet soup,
a ladle stirring its deep flavors,
each bowl filled to the rim.
There was still enough time

to have held dirt,
Everything has a trace of divine in it.
Mother had instructed us to burn
her body when the time came,

as if we could summon a mob
of drunken fireflies to swab discreetly
her evaporating soul like perfume.
For her, they'd do this favor.

She was that close to nature.
Such privileges had nothing
to do with money—but if they did,
no one dared mention it

(damned if we did) except, finally,
my sister, who felt her *ch'i*
was strong enough to handle it.
The priest agreed to bless Mother's ashes

with or without a service.
But there had to be a casket
to shelter any hope of a Resurrection.
Rented, used, it was awful—as well

as a waste. The priest agreed, but it
was still a rule. Later that night,
I asked my sister's husband,
who loved working with his hands,

if he could hammer a wooden box
out of pine boards. Afterwards,
my sister added, my husband and I
could easily transport Mother

to Byesville, Ohio.
That's just the kind of thing
Ford pickups are great for.
I snapped back *no way.*

Mother was going in their Volvo.
She hated any kind of ceremony,
everyone pretending to feel bad.
And didn't she once say that funerals

made her laugh, not knowing why.
Neither did we, not sure if she
was ill or cool and if it was genetic.
I don't know how in life we find

ourselves unrecognizable, how pain
pushes us to survive despite ourselves.
I don't know how it comes to burying
those who, in the end, outlive us all—

those whom we can't live without,
lightly pressing his or her hand
against our face,
asking for forgiveness,

how every night before I fall
into my room's deep well
I turn toward good intentions,
well-placed collection envelopes,

worn jackets off my back,
spiders glowing approval
in the dark while it rains outside,
how despite ourselves,

we fuck up what we love most,
trying to uncover the God in us
as we sift through each day
so desperate, so hungry, so cheap.

Tulips

What good is love?
My mother's hand shakes

as she offers it to me
for a goodnight kiss.

I know only hunger,
the wind between my ribs

that will not add weight,
the scales frozen;

heavenly body meant
for someone else.

She whispers: *Ja tebe lybly*,
I love you,

into the phone
knowing an ocean heaves

between us—our blood
breathes daughter

mirrored into sister,
Father invisible,

calming the curtain;
proof he lives.

Each morning the vase
next to my mother's bed

darkens water into earth.
No one will find them there.

What is your favorite memory, Mother?
I cannot paint it.

What is your favorite flower?
Two lips in the dark.

December

1.

Dear   ,

Holding her was like holding a large fallen leaf,
her hair recently dyed an unnatural red
perhaps the russet of Ohio's steel mills.

This moment didn't last long;
embarrassed, she pushed me away.
I kept my sunglasses on,

recalling her *You don't look good*
when you cry.

2.

Dear   ,

Ten minutes of storm pass over the lake, knocking
dead branches off trees, pushing water.

Her phone lies sideways on her bed.
Long-distance voices disappear in marsh grass,

It's your daughter spills
out of the receiver—

She turns it upright as if it were a vase.

3.

Dear   ,

A blue piece of paper dropped from my Grandmother's hands
onto the wooden floor of our house.

She died years ago, buoyant, among the fire burning
in my dream, through my mother's waking

screams, grass fields rippling not toward
but away from our house.

Have faith, faith will protect you

Where did it come from? On my floor?

4.

Dear   ,

*I'm just trying to get to heaven, and I think I'm getting
closer*

a man mumbles past me
in the treatment room.

Others, too—children
wearing startled adult masks

& still others waiting to be born,
for me to vacate my chair.

5.

Dear   ,

They could've carried you on their shoulders
for hours, your body rocking gently

from side to side as if in a boat.

Before they closed you for eternity,
I saw your thumbs move,

but not enough.

6.

Dear   ,

Be still,

ants cast lions' shadows to entertain themselves,

branches scrape music
against windows,

each day prognosticated—

living as if.

III

Lava Lamp

Fifty, the ultimate *"F word"* to these punks
pricing lava lamps and crossbones,

confusing thick leather wristbands
for passion's steel thorns.

No one but me takes notice of the ease
with which they assign death to their own

idiosyncratic dark. My raw health, too,
wears shark-fin gelled hair—shabby-sexy

in a beanbag chair kind of way.
An incense stick threads smoke

aisles away from wind-up chattering teeth
not unlike the dentures my mother pulled

from her mouth to startle my young
children when she baby-sat, once.

Yesterday, my blood, sweet string of mood lights,
abandoned me for a hung 100 watt bulb

and flickering neon tongue; the new
hardware of my dream basement

where a waterbed heaves welcome
in wafts of watered-down beer.

Pin our lips together; play my words
backwards: see if they say I'm alive.

Paper Cut

Thin-boned, thin-skinned, I make
my way on an even thinner path,

leaves crumbling like torn brown backs
of frames, mats removed, glass broken,

scattered in the woods. The sun seeps
yolk-yellow but today I only see

starved cows on hillsides
pebbles trickled with water.

I survive my own self-portrait.
The smallest red tear of skin

sends my body's temperature up.
My daughter, Raisa, wearily sleeps in front

of the wood burning stove,
the flame on the log sputtering,

like an angry muscleman, she insists,
pounding his way out.

Martini Glass

"A perfect breast is shaped like an inverted
martini glass," my father liked to say,

"the nipple, a dark grape
or more like an olive . . . ."

Was that what he was thinking
when he posed naked for my mother's camera,

lying on their bed, a crystal glass
raised high in the air,

a private toast to himself
for having realized something so important?

After his death, my mother cut off
the bottom half of the photograph

before burying it in the family's
leather chest.

She didn't want the kids
to remember him erect,

readjusting the flood lamps—
just a face, transfixed,

as if he'd just been shot
with a tranquilizing dart.

The Fitting

Pulling the curtain closed, Diana, the consultant,
carefully places before me each beige knoll

diminishing in size from turtle shell
to as small as a pincushion.

The black sports bra doesn't come in my
You're so petite, your ribs tiny as a child's! size

but pockets can be custom-sewn into anything—
evening dresses, silver sequined as a winter sky.

She says the ladies like to laugh a little
when several weeks after surgery they come

for an hour fitting, leave feeling more
like their old selves, a temporary

complimentary *poof* to slip into swimsuits,
a flesh-colored traveling case

to carry their new *accommodation* in.
It's okay to get it wet but not okay

to leave it out where a dog can get to it.
One boy left alone for the night

tried biting into one after stealing it out
of his mother's special, secret drawer.

She nods, symmetry *is* important.
But in your case, standing a few feet back,

squinting one eye, *you're the closest to a boy
I've ever seen.* I let her laugh, do her job.

Now she cups it carefully in the palm of her hand
It needs to be fed . . . .

How believably plump it feels.
I want to take turns . . . place

the powdered smooth side
against her cheek.

Convertible Night

I want to say I laughed and it felt good,
that the hairdresser laughed along,
and the lady waiting for a cut after me
didn't look horrified, then away,

but that day I'd just gotten the nerve up
to go get a trim for my auburn wig.

He cut it fashionably
shorter, holding the small oval
mirror up to its perfect, *just a touch*,
sprayed dome.

Even after I told him *Thank you, it's lovely, fine*,
he couldn't resist switching

to his extra-wide brush
for that one flourishing final swoop,
catching the scalp netting
and pulling the wig off my head.

It hung from his brush
like a snagged fish on a line,

until I quickly tugged it back,
patted it and stared ahead,
unable to even smile,
move, almost mute.

After tipping him, I disappeared
into my room, fully dressed, back to bed.

My wig and I lie cheek to cheek
on my bed, bangs softly swept to the right.
O convertible night,
stars above my Styrofoam head.

The Cop

I wasn't the sassy redhead he thought he'd pulled over,
black-framed designer sunglasses hiding the fire in her eyes,

whose car he'd walked extra slow to,
passenger window lowering as she turned to speak,

ice slipping from the safety glass as from a square fin,
hiding deep inside the car door, smudge-less, ready to rise.

He looked directly at my mouth to see what it might
be, a warm, welcoming silence, or a dog caught with a bone.

But my lips are too thin, slightly purple like morning
glories choking along their white line.

His hands were large. He spread his legs, ripped the ticket
out of his book as if he was about to strip and the ticket

was the first accessory to go. No, I wasn't the woman
he thought he pulled over, but a spinning out of control

strip show coming right back at him. I pulled off my wig, held
it out to him like a scalp, a sacrifice, an enormous spider mashed

on the dashboard. *Holy Jesus*, he muttered, *sorry, sorry, sorry*,
stepping back from my car. He didn't know where to look—

no eyelashes, no brows, no face to match the face
on the driver's license, no deep sky blue backdrop curtain

to highlight the eyes. My hands shook on the steering wheel.
A woman can be dismantled, yet she moves or dies—

the cop is thankful his kids or his wife are not me,
this woman for whom he now wishes Godspeed toward

her prayers or the mother ship or the ocean's white lip,
his large hand holding back traffic as together we pull out,

gravel kicking up from behind his tires,
siren blasting birds like torn paper wavering in the air.

By nightfall I'll convince myself it is a gift:
this life so thick it sticks deep in my throat

parched and yellowing, overgrown shoulder
like weeds rippling throughout my body—

the cop home and showered with a story to tell,
his family gathered inside their dinner halo.

Ballet on Chemo

1.

an usher touched my elbow, whispered

I was all of *that*, pointing to the lit stage,
only standing still.

2.

I've watched young dancers on break
in the theatre's back alley,

bitter, hungry snowflakes huddled
in December rain smoking Marlboros.

3.

My oncologist says *Sure, why not*

bend back to a time
when I could bend,

my neck and shoulders like tree boughs.

The scarf wrapped low on my forehead
translates into high cheekbones, eyes

dark-circled by Russian winters.

4.

The ballet mistress smiles at me,
then, after that, pretends not to see

what's too much to correct.

5.

Each week I re-write my blood,
white cells like young swans with silver crowns

rushing out of black backdrops,
rushing in.

All Gone

Among first words kids learn to say
tipping their empty bowls and sipping cups.

After that, Disney producers remind them
moms, too, have to go—

on hospital beds, in mall accidents,
just before a rodeo.

Dads remain strong in plaid flannel shirts
capable of handling a combine, moving everyone

to the country to begin again, the neighbor,
Not Mom, new to town (or not)—

maybe the town's longstanding vet,
sensitive with horses, stroking their long necks

& more like a friend. She knows she's not Mom,
who, except for being dead, is always present

in the wind-gusted silk fluff of milkweed pod.
After dinner, Not Mom tucks the kids in.

She doesn't have to check her weight or blood
or kick the bucket on Lifetime Channel.

Not Mom knows when it's time to give it all a break.
She turns toward Dad, lowers the heat under the kettle.

Sea Gull

Whether the mackerel was holy
is forgotten the way all bad jokes

are forgotten, hung in the back
of closets like old coats,

silk linings snagged.
The horizon separating blue from blue

kept the sea gull hooked on our line,
a kite, alive, pulling upward

toward the sky's blinding clarity.
My husband and I motored

our small red boat around
the inlet named *Spit*—

a red slash of bait
in our pail.

The more I pulled, the more
it pulled back, hook in its beak,

riding the sky, its white wings
blocking the sun,

strips of light bending
like wheat in the wind.

Our Long Shadows

for Jay

You too notice the danger—and turn
like an alien slowly pointing

to the passing school of fish
changing direction quicker than the wind.

It's hard to believe the hand
that destroys creates, that floating

facedown, my loose legs
kneel before what could be God.

The Great Barracuda beneath us
doesn't move, paralyzed

by a single thought
occupying its entire body

or perhaps only sleeping
no matter how furiously we wave,

the masks pressing our faces
into a constant *oh!*

Our long shadows
skim the ocean floor,

anxieties dissolve from our bodies.
Free, afloat, we look across

warm salty water to the yellow
umbrella shimmering on our veranda

where you in white drank red,
and I in red drank white.

IV

—Take a moment, just one, and when its fine shell,
Two joined palms, slowly opens
What do you see?

—Czeslaw Milosz,
"A Frivolous Conversation"

Owl—*Cyva*

I.

I translated from dusk its wings, the black sails
    of exacting eyes,

feathers snow-speckled, talons hooking
    a long oak branch.

I translated my opened hands into light
    against a bare March sky,

the heat of splintered wood. I breathed in,
    exhaled a gray feather

fallen across a winter meadow
    in which a house would be built,

its family asleep behind a closed door.
    I breathed in *hare*,

exhaled an exclamation mark
    before turning the page.

II.

And in a first dream of spring floods,
    the frogs cry-croak, roused by water,

and through the sound of rain, more rain—
    a house mushrooming,

its family asleep under the first blank page,
    winter following rain,

mice carrying grain. Inside, a warming stove,
    night floating like a feather

becoming *moon* outside my window,
    before the window opened into *voice*

and *voice* into a fox's throat, and *I*
        a feather that could not be named.

III.

Eyes of a woman drowned in her tub, Solomea,
        in Kiev, on the eve of the new millennium,

at the mouth of a river I know only by *Desna*—
        bones, hair, the disk of her face.

I call her *Cyva*, a nocturnal bird, heard her song.
        I raise the oars of a small canoe

and see a man, a friend, Ed, look up
        through water, a notebook still

in his hand, his eyes moving, as if reading—
        the shadow of a willow

that buries him. I took to my lips
        the language of my mother, father,

sister, the language of birds
        hemmed in a tree at night outside a room

where I read waiting for the river,
        for words that would hunt by night.

Wolves

To touch the back of such a man—
my mother whispers—*Of course*

it means he belongs to a club
that has sex with wolves—

a wolf's paw prints tattooed
upward to the right of his spine—

Don't be so naïve.
His secret trail hidden from patients,

how vivid the unseen,
the nape of his neck—

a few stray curls, underbrush.
He hands me pink dumbbells.

How many women has he seen
like me, avalanched, quick

to turn from mirrors?
On the bench press, my

right arm buckles in;
too much has been cut away.

You're so tiny, he says—code for
slight, small-boned, soft-spoken,

wish-boned, muscle-deprived?
But I know how some wolves

never get past hunger,
ribs stabbing through their

blotch-gray fur.
Into the first clearing

they run, head down.
Sunken deep into the cold

they'll rip ice from their paws
as if hard water alone could feed them.

White Orchard

I remind myself:
one day we wear the faces we deserve.
Where would they go without us?
Paw raised, the neighbor's dog's eyes
are suspiciously dark.

Once we cherished them,
their uncanny resemblance
of dog to master,
owner to same
square-jawed house,
moustache to eyebrow.
We didn't stray far
from each photograph's
black-and-white orchard,
almost-ripe faces of cousins.

In another life, I would've followed them
to my mother's room
where she looks up at me,
prophetically lifts her finger
to a paper cup knocked over.

I see what she names in me now:
scant grasses, a radiation of birds.

Inherited

probably an emptied showcase
liquor cabinet
lit from inside,

a laboriously hand-painted egg
displayed like a portrait
fragile, vacant—
a pinhole, still intact, to blow into.

Carpe Diem

A fly sticks to a strip, its life work.
In *Hidden Acres*, the town's new development,

a man tests a chain saw
against a hunk of tree.

I drive the long way around
anything that reminds me

of myself—
easy sweets, the greasy,

screaming *open all night* restaurants
of my middle-aged blood.

A motorcycle cuts across
the day's pale lawn

leaving behind an empty helmet,
its rider passed into oblivion.

In my daughter's room
sand dollar chimes drop onto the windowsill

while two hermit crabs
inch toward a damp sponge,

a bright green peace sign painted on one shell,
a Harley flame on the other.

Not Quite

1.

Not quite hidden behind the wicker chair,
Mother pulls her gray wool skirt

down around her ankles.
She stands in her loose diaper.

Not quite hidden behind the wicker chair,
She steps out of her skirt

as if stepping out of a fountain.

2.

But how can I deny her
the many skirts she brings,

the kitchen floor opening up
like a meadow for her?

My pee-pee like spring rain . . . .

Deny her?

How wonderful
to run a wet washcloth up
between my legs,

run a second, dry one
down to my knees.

It's art, she reminds me, to know you're clean.

Good Cells

Make them as true as Father
pointing to heaven knowing
he's left no one behind,
tenacious as my mother
looking out a window at a lone
resident tree. Hand her a paintbrush.
Let her drag its bristled hair
across a white page.
Let them carry my husband's
snow-dampened wood,
be the passing flickering flashlight.
Let them be my son
and my daughter, the scent of white soap.
Let them be my working dog, Laika,
the flurry of stones as we walked.
Let them sound for my sister
Monday's church bells,
a piano's felt-covered hammers,
her husband's throat, nine years cancer-free.
Let them carry light suitcases
to my nephew and niece
in industrious cities,
where they may
applaud fruit ripening on a table
without its tree.

The Carnegie Mellon Poetry Series Backlist 2002–2008

2002
Among the Musk Ox People, Mary Ruefle
The Memphis Letters, Jay Meek
What it Wasn't, Laura Kasischke
The Finger Bone, Kevin Prufer
The Late World, Arthur Smith
Slow Risen Among the Smoke Trees, Elizabeth Kirschner
Keeping Time, Suzanne Cleary
Astronaut, Brian Henry

2003
Imitation of Life, Allison Joseph
A Place Made of Starlight, Peter Cooley
The Mastery Impulse, Ricardo Pau-Llosa
Except for One Obscene Brushstroke, Dzvinia Orlowsky
Taking Down the Angel, Jeff Friedman
Casino of the Sun, Jerry Williams
Trouble, Mary Baine Campbell
Lives of Water, John Hoppenthaler

2004
Freeways and Aqueducts, James Harms
Tristimania, Mary Ruefle
Prague Winter, Richard Katrovas
Venus Examines Her Breast, Maureen Seaton
Trains in Winter, Jay Meek
The Women Who Loved Elvis All Their Lives, Fleda Brown
The Chronic Liar Buys a Canary, Elizabeth Edwards
Various Orbits, Thom Ward

2005
Laws of My Nature, Margot Schilpp
Things I Can't Tell You, Michael Dennis Browne
Renovation, Jeffrey Thomson
Sleeping Woman, Herbert Scott
Blindsight, Carol Hamilton
Fallen from a Chariot, Kevin Prufer
Needlegrass, Dennis Sampson
Bent to the Earth, Blas Manuel De Luna

2006
Burn the Field, Amy Beeder
Dog Star Delicatessen: New and Selected Poems 1979-2006,
    Mekeel McBride
The Sadness of Others, Hayan Charara
A Grammar to Waking, Nancy Eimers
Shinemaster, Michael McFee
Eastern Mountain Time, Joyce Peseroff
Dragging the Lake, Robert Thomas

2007
So I Will Till the Ground, Gregory Djanikian
Trick Pear, Suzanne Cleary
Indeed I Was Pleased with the World, Mary Ruefle
The Situation, John Skoyles
One Season Behind, Sarah Rosenblatt
The Playhouse Near Dark, Elizabeth Holmes
Drift and Pulse, Kathleen Halme
Black Threads, Jeff Friedman
On the Vanishing of Large Creatures, Susan Hutton

2008
The Grace of Necessity, Samuel Green
After West, James Harms
The Book of Sleep, Eleanor Stanford
Anticipate the Coming Reservoir, John Hoppenthaler
Parable Hunter, Ricardo Pau-Llosa
Convertible Night, Flurry of Stones, Dzvinia Orlowsky

← barcode